Breaking the Rules

D0533467

Dedicated with love to John,
Charlie and Josh

Breaking the rules

Coral Rumble

Illustrated by Nigel Baines

LION
CHILDREN'S

Text copyright © 2004 Coral Rumble
Illustrations copyright © 2004 Nigel Baines
This edition copyright © 2004 Lion Hudson

The moral rights of the author and illustrator
have been asserted

A Lion Children's Book
an imprint of
Lion Hudson plc
Mayfield House, 256 Banbury Road,
Oxford OX2 7DH, England
www.lionhudson.com
ISBN-13: 978-0-7459-4857-7
ISBN-10: 0-7459-4857-X

First edition 2004
10 9 8 7 6 5 4 3

All rights reserved

Acknowledgments
Poems on pages 14, 93 first published in *The Works*, Paul Cookson (ed.), Macmillan,
2000; 25 first published in *Christmas Poems*, Gaby Morgan (ed.), Macmillan, 2003;
26 published in *The Rhyme Riot*, Gaby Morgan (ed.), Macmillan, 2002; 27 first
published in *Fire Words*, John Foster (ed.), OUP, 2000; 30, 45 published in *Pet Poems*,
Jennifer Curry (ed.), Scholastic, 2001; 33 published in *Funny Poems*, Jan Dean
(ed.), Scholastic, 2003; 40 published in *Ridiculous Rhymes*, John Foster (ed.),
Collins, 2002; 48 'Sometimes', published in *The Works 2*, Brian Moses and Pie
Corbett (eds), Macmillan, 2002; 50 'Gran Fan' published in *Fantastic Football Poems*,
John Foster (ed.), OUP, 2001, and 'Holiday Print' published in *Funny Poems*, Jan
Dean (ed.), Scholastic, 2003; 54 'Sum Haiku' published in 'Poetry Forms' posters,
David Harmer (ed.), Folens, 1999; 66 published in *Bonkers for Conkers*, Gaby Morgan
(ed.), Macmillan, 2003; 68 published in *Mice on Ice*, Gaby Morgan (ed.), Macmillan,
2004; 78 published in *Eccentric Epitaphs*, John Foster (ed.), Collins, 2002; 83
published in *Writing Poetry: Book 1*, David Orme (ed.), Badger Publishing, 2002; 90
published in *You're Not Going Out Like That!*, Paul Cookson (ed.), Macmillan, 2003;
95 published in *Football Fever*, John Foster (ed.), OUP, 2000; 96 published in *Don't
Get Your Knickers in a Twist*, Paul Cookson (ed.), Macmillan, 2002.

A catalogue record for this book is available
from the British Library

Typeset in 12/14 Latin 725 BT
Printed and bound in Great Britain
by Cox & Wyman Ltd, Reading

Contents

Introduction

Grown-ups sometimes say that rules are there to be broken – which can be their way of getting themselves out of trouble! It's true that some rules are a bit silly, so we find ourselves saying things like, 'I can't believe it!' and, 'How stupid is that!' But did you know that our amazing world runs on rules too? Rules designed to keep everything working together, and I'm sure we wouldn't want any of those rules broken!

Breaking the Rules is full of poems where rules have been broken. Some of them are about subjects that we, as a rule, avoid – like death, prejudice, baboons' bottoms and Grandad's pants!

Many poems break the rules of traditional poetry. Some are written in free verse, without regular rhythm or rhyme. Others are shape poems or calligram poems*, where the way the letters are formed is an important part of the poem. You will also find poems that are a bit like word sculptures. Grown-ups call these concrete poems**, although they're really not heavy!

Of course, there are poems in this book about breaking the rules in everyday life. Some will stretch your imagination – like shrinking teachers (very

---

*A poem in which calligraphy (the way letters are formed or the font used) represents the poem's subject, or part of it – for example, a poem about being scared might be written in shaky letters. 'Cats can' is a calligram poem.
**A poem in which the layout of the words represents an aspect of the subject. Visual art and language work together in this kind of poem. 'Isolated' is a concrete poem.

naughty!), a duck eating in a restaurant (very unhygienic!); while others are about real situations – like breaking your friends' rules when they're wrong (very brave).

Last but not least, a few poems look at the consequences of breaking rules – like getting a detention, a plant dying when it's not been watered, or what your conscience does to you if you cheat.

So, sit back and enjoy a little bit of naughtiness mixed with a few deep thoughts – poets can't resist that sort of thing!

P.S. To set the scene, the book kicks off with some verses about a badly behaved poem breaking school rules!

A poem flew at me, it did

A poem flew at me, it did,
It wriggled down my pen,
Slid itself out of the nib
To see the world again.

It danced into a rhythm,
Its hips swung to and fro
As rhymes and pictures grew in lines –
I just went with the flow.

When the poem filled the page,
I read it back to me,
And marvelled that such romping words
Had come to me for free.

My teacher said, 'Let's dance,
Your poem's got me moving.'
And so the class danced out of school
In an ecstasy of grooving.

A policeman put his hand up,
Said, 'Stop this jiggling now!'
Teacher said, 'We'd like to stop
But we just don't know how!'

'This poem has us captured,
It's sliding through our veins,
It rushes round our bodies
And then goes round again.'

The policeman's foot was tapping
And then his hips swung low,
The rhythm had seeped through his pores
And we had him in tow.

My teacher said, 'Stop writing!
The head will have me sacked.'
But words kept flowing from my pen,
I couldn't hold them back.

Before too long the poem's beat
Was stomping through the town,
And echoing refrains
Were bouncing up and down.

But when night fell, to our relief,
The poem flew away
Into the night sky, to a star,
Where rebel poems play.

Nature

Cats can

Cats can s t r e t c h

And cats can curl

Cats can p o u n c e

And t w i r l and t w i r l

Cats can ^s^ it

z
z
z

And cats can laze

And purr into

A sleepy haze

Kangaroos cannot knit

Kangaroos cannot knit;
Clinical tests have been done.
If you put a kangaroo alone in a room
With a pair of knitting needles
And a ball of wool,
It will not knit.
It will bounce,
It will scratch,
It will stare with the snooty air of a camel,
But it will not knit.

They've experimented with many different
    colours of wool
But the result is the same.
Dark colours, bright colours, glowing in the
    night colours –
None of them move a kangaroo to knit.
It's been proved, absolutely.
Not a shadow of doubt.
Kangaroos cannot knit.

It's almost as if they weren't designed for it!

Moth cave

I once caught a moth
And placed it in a brown paper bag,
Blown up and roomy.
Inside flutters tickled the bag belly,
A quiet scratching on a strong wall of stiff paper –
A bag of brown fidgeting,
Of sweeping circles
And trembling arcs,
So light but full of living.
Scared of cruelty, I gently pulled open the bag mouth,
Looked into the cave and blew.
The moth rushed past my cheek
Like a brittle leaf on a windy day.

The intruder

On this hot, sunny afternoon,
When the classroom feels like a glassroom
Fitted out for torture,
I'm kept awake by an intruder.

Buzz buzz buzz.
The teacher's voice drones on,
Each syllable fainter than the one before.
But the buzzing gets louder,
Buzz buzz buzz buzz buzz.
I watch him fly and land, fly and land,
A black, jiggling dot on the blind,

On the window,

On the ceiling,

On my desk.

He walks his jittery way across my exercise book,
Transparent wings folded like a lady's fan,
Until buzz buzz buzz buzz,
He zips towards an open window and leaves,
Without any apology for the interruption.

Red fox

Red fox

    leaves a trail

        where he has stepped

    this snowy morning

        leaving his

    frozen scent nesting

        in the holes

    of his paw prints

Memorial

When our dog died
Memories wagged in my head,
Backwards and forwards.
My mind was alive with
Pictures of him running, rolling, resting.
I could hear him bark,
His crazy back-door scratching,
His lapping tongue, splashing.

His collar, so empty now,
Hangs in the kitchen
Like a memorial plaque,
Reminding us he once lived here.
And sometimes, as I pass by,
I run my fingers over it,
Stroking the memories
Until I find a smile.

Shadowman

I play an eerie darkness tune,
Snuff out the sun and light the moon,
Then steal beach-yellow from each dune,
Shadowman is here.

I suck the green from every tree,
Drink the blue of lake and sea,
Fade the black and gold of bee,
Shadowman is here.

I smudge the butterfly to grey,
Wipe the red of fox away,
Drain the colours of the day,
Shadowman is here.

You say I'm just a trick of light,
A disappearing act at night,
And yet you always get a fright
When Shadowman is here!

Bright sparks

y

a

w

a

t

a

o

l

f

t

a

h

t

s

k

r

a

p

s

of
to let go
they're forced
spit and hiss as
lose their splintered grip,
but clawing, wooden fingers
hums a tune of destruction –
crackles a cackle of hot delight
holds tightly with its orange glow,
→ the furnace heart of the fire consumes –

Fire dragon

The flames leap high,
Just then I spy a dragon
As green as the moss
On the wood that we burn on the fire.

His nose is smudged with ash dust;
He spits and hisses
From his tiger-orange lair.

Fragile coals crack under the weight
Of his ballooning stomach,
Crumble as his tail sweeps the grate.

Flame points prick
And climb his craggy back and head –
His eyes glow red with anger.

I leave him, safely trapped
Behind the guard, to pace and glare,
And I stare back at my book,

The words jumble, my mind wanders
Off to a land of castles and tall towers.

The night sky – Christmas Eve

Is this the same star
they saw from afar
Is this the same light
that shone that night
Is this the same glow
that made them know
Is this the same spark
that never grows dark

?

In a forest clearing

Pine tree in the forest,
Standing tall.
Water dripping from needles
Like crystal baubles –
Exploding on the forest floor
Like fairy lights.
Waiting.

The first bit

I love the first bit of the morning,
The bit of the day that no one has used yet,
The part that is so clean
You must wipe your feet before you walk out into it.
The bit that smells like rose petals and cut grass
And dampens your clothes with dew.

If you go out, you will bump into secrets,
Discover miracles usually covered by bus fumes.
You will hear pure echoes, whispers and scuttling.

I love the first bit of the morning
When the sun has only one eye open
And the day is like a clean shirt,
Uncreased and ready to put on;
The part that gets your attention
By being so quiet.

Egg

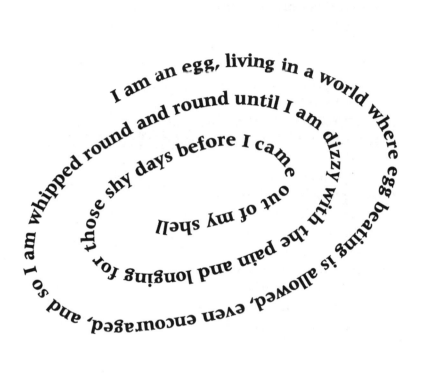

I am an egg, living in a world where egg beating is allowed, even encouraged, and so I am whipped round and round until I am dizzy with the pain and longing for those shy days before I came out of my shell

The pet lover's prayer

For wagging tails
And big brown eyes,
For silky ears
And whining cries,

For perfect poise
And darting feet,
For curls and stretches
And sudden leaps,

For teeth that gnaw
And wheels that spin,
For long, thin tails
As limp as string,

For noses that twitch
And well-toothed gums,
For ears that flop
And soft, small tums,

For beaks that squawk
And perches that swing,
For colours that shout
And dance and sing,

For all of these
And for all the fun
In house and garden,
In cage and run,
We thank you God.

Pet shop rap

We've got a pet shop,
A noisy pet shop,
A chirping, barking pet shop.
We've got a pet shop,
A lively pet shop,
A splashing, dashing pet shop.

We've got...
Tiny gerbils,
Purring cats,
Cute little puppies,
Black and white rats,
Birds that sing,
Mice that squeak,
Hairy black spiders,
Parrots that speak.

We've got a pet shop,
A noisy pet shop,
A chirping, barking pet shop.
We've got a pet shop,
A lively pet shop,
A splashing, dashing pet shop.

We've got…
Swimming turtles,
Darting fish,
Guinea pigs
Sitting in their dish,
Hamsters that nibble,
Snakes that glide,
Rabbits that bounce,
Lizards that hide.

We've got a pet shop,
A noisy pet shop,
A chirping, barking pet shop.
We've got a pet shop,
A lively pet shop,
A splashing, dashing pet shop.

Baboons' bottoms

Baboons' bottoms
Are so rude,
Red and shiny
And so nude;
Lumpy, bumpy,
With a laugh
They flash them
For each photograph!

Baboons' bottoms,
Bright and lewd,
Blue and yucky,
Oh so crude!
I think my aunt
Would be more happy
If they were made
To wear a nappy!

Baboons' bottoms,
What a sight!
Designed to give
Your gran a fright;
Who can't believe
The age-old rumour
That God has got
A sense of humour!

Restaurant bill

A duck walked into a restaurant
And everybody stared
(Other ducks had wanted to
But none had ever dared).

He sat down at a table,
Put a napkin on his lap,
Then motioned to a waiter
Who got in quite a flap.

The waiter said, 'Excuse me, Sir,
You seem to be a duck…
I'm not allowed to serve you,
You'll have to leave, bad luck!'

The duck took a deep breath
Then spoke in tones composed,
'I see no sign to that effect,
So that's the matter closed.'

'I'm sorry, Sir,' the waiter said,
'You really can't eat here...
I believe there is a perfect spot
Just down beside the weir.'

'OK,' said the duck, 'I must admit
I came in for a dare.'
And with that he winked and waddled out
With his bill held in the air.

Duck fight!

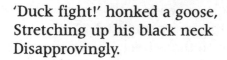

'Duck fight!' honked a goose,
Stretching up his black neck
Disapprovingly.

'Duck fight!' shrilled a great crested grebe,
Preening and fluffing
Nervously.

'Duck fight!' whispered a mandarin duck,
Blushing and twitching
Awkwardly.

'Duck fight!' croaked a moorhen,
Red face shield glowing
Excitedly.

'Duck fight!' called a coot,
White face paling
Anxiously.

And, sure enough,
Reeds parted to a frenzied flush of tail feathers,
Soft, salmon-pink mouths pushed wide, hard, yellow
　　bills,
Quacks and whistles cut the air,
Suspending all bird-call as anger splashed from bank
　　to bank.

Life sentence

BEHIND THE BARS   the tiger's eyes   BEHIND THE BARS   the tiger's eyes   BEHIND THE BARS

Show deep, deep longing and deep, deep scars

Coconuts

the branches stretch out

and out and out hanging heavy with

co co nuts

up
and
up
and
up
stretch
trees
palm

Plant care

not
did
I
it
water
but
pot
a
inside
plant
a
grew
I

so
as
you
see
it
droops
its
head
and
I
suspect
the
plant
is

dead

Seal of approval

A seal walked into a health farm
And sat on the counter to speak:
'I want to lose pounds of this blubber,
Could you book me in for a week?

My skirts are all tight round the middle,
My blouses feel *so* teeny-weeny,
With my midriff so wibbly and wobbly
I'm embarrassed to wear my bikini!'

The staff found a personal trainer
And a diet for blubber removal,
And were happy to find at the end of the week
That they'd got a seal of approval!

Silver pool silence

One night I stared into a silver pool,
Looking down and down
Into the inky-black deep.
Trees surrounded the pool,
Their moon-shadows cracking the silver surface.
It was so quiet.
Even the night owl held his breath,
And a water boatman froze in position –
Counting his heartbeats in the silence.
Nothing in nature was awkward;
Every tiny, creeping thing knew it belonged.
God smiled
And a playful breeze rumpled the pool surface
Like a father ruffling the hair of his child.

Big bang mystery

When I've been running in a field,
Through the long tangle-round-my-legs grass,
There's nothing better than collapsing
Onto the bug-ridden ground, to stare up at the sky,
The blue, blue sky, as clear as an angel's conscience.

On days when there are no clouds
I scan the perfect arc and breathe in
The spotless air – deeply, deeply.
On days when there are clouds
(Pure, white poodle froth)
I let my imagination wander around the shapes,
Until my eyes see something magical.

Sometimes I sit up,
Whistle through grass at circling birds,
Before running to a favourite tree –
Old and wise with rings of years.
And, sometimes, I sink to the ground,
In the shade of its huge, barky arms
And listen to field music.

Afterwards, when I know I should get home,
I walk with fresh steps,
Wondering how a big bang could end like this.

Jellyfish fuss

When I was a child I stood on a rock
For fear of stepping on jellyfish.

The beach was littered with them
And I feared the sting of the tentacles,
The jelly of the saucers.

The rock was warm and firm;
Like a castle it lifted me above danger.

I closed my eyes, curled up and listened
To distant waves raking the shingle,
And seagulls chuckling, 'Auk-auk-auk.'

The tide was coming in, it was time to move,
But how, when jellyfish waited and wobbled?

Two large hands clasped my waist,
I flew up into the salty air,
Saved by Dad, who picked his way through
    the jellyfish
Like a carnival stilt-walker.

My stick insect is hiding

w e q
n
s
l
t
r
y
m
a
v
h
s
i
t
c
e
s
n
i
k
c
i
t
s
y
m

b
o
l
j
g
c
i d i n g j u s t h e r e

h d h f o m g h e
k y
f t
b w e r f h t i s z e

45

Dazzle

layer upon layer, snow covers the hillside with the dazzle of purity

layer upon layer, snow covers the hillside with the dazzle of

layer upon layer, snow covers the hillside with the dazzle

layer upon layer, snow covers the hillside with the

layer upon layer, snow covers the hillside with

layer upon layer, snow covers the hillside

layer upon layer, snow covers the

layer upon layer, snow covers

layer upon layer, snow

layer upon layer,

layer upon

→ layer

A Pick of
Poem Patterns
(Say that quickly!)

Sad school cinquains

DIFFERENT
Jodie
Is different
And so she sits alone.
She never looks up from her desk
To smile.

QUIET
Miss Law
Looks sad today,
She is quiet and still.
Her grown-up world has followed her
To school.

TESTS
In tests
I get low marks.
My teacher says, 'Well tried,'
But her words don't mean anything
To me.

SOMETIMES
Sometimes
They just stare hard,
Nudge each other and smile;
And I pretend that I don't care –
Sometimes.

STANDING
Standing
By the office,
In trouble once again,
Makes my heart bash against my ribs
Loudly.

A line of limericks

MID-LIFE CRISIS
A middle-aged teacher from Poole
Thought his dancing was groovy and cool;
At the end-of-term disco
He slipped out a disc, oh...
How he did hobble round school!

GRAN FAN
A soccer-mad gran from Dundee
Served her club from breakfast 'til tea;
She sold programmes and stickers,
Knitted team-colour knickers,
And crocheted the goal nets for free!

HOLIDAY PRINT
There was a young man from Dundee
Who had a great passion to ski;
He skied with aggression,
And left an impression –
The shape of himself on a tree!

HOUSE ARREST
There once was a child politician
Who set out on a pest control mission;
He banned adult faces
From all public places,
Until they came under submission!

TUMMY TROUBLE

A school dinner lady from Rhyl
Was out on a mission to kill:
Her first course was chewy,
The gravy quite gluey,
And the pudding made everyone ill.

A huddle of haiku

EARLY MORNING HAIKU
Quiet, stirring day,
A leaf flaps, dripping dewdrops,
Schoolboys shiver by.

BOY BAND HAIKU
Boy bands strut the stage
Until they're out of season,
Fashion's wind cuts deep.

ANSWERS
At the end of prayers
God waits, silently thinking,
Weighing his answers.

CLASS THIEF
Own up! Who's got it?
There's a syllable missing
From Daniel's hai

(OK, give that one back too!)

A CONVENIENT HAIKU
The toilet seat's up,
Dad's really in trouble now –
Marriage guidance time!

SUM HAIKU

All my sums are wrong,
I wish I could go home now.
Raindrops wash my face.

SUNBURN HAIKU

Ouch, ouch, ouch, ouch, ouch;
Red, hot skin peels and blisters,
Cool cream lies like snow.

HAIKU FOR LOSERS

When my team loses
I walk home without speaking.
Each sigh hurts my chest.

HOW HIGH CAN YOU HAIKU?

Hai hai hai hai hai
And up, and over, and down,
Ku ku ku ku ku!

Human Nature

Breaking the rules

When Nadia started at our school
Miss said she should join our table,
But she didn't, she couldn't –
She sat with us, but apart,
Nobody let her in –
That would be breaking the rules.
Friends have rules to keep others out,
To let them know they're not part of things.

Nadia had an accent,
It marked her out.
Lucy said, 'People with accents can't join us,
It's against the rules.'
Rachel said, 'Shy people can't join us,
It's against the rules.'
Gemma said, 'People who aren't from round here
Have different rules.'

But on Saturday I saw Nadia in the park,
Pushing backwards and forwards on a swing,
Her feet still on the ground – with her heart.
When she saw me I noticed her melt into nothing.
Sorry seemed a small word.
'D'you want a push?' I asked.
Nadia smiled in a language I knew.
We spent all afternoon laughing and messing about
Breaking the rules.

Just a skin thing

This is the skin
That I've grown up in.
I've filled every part
And look pretty smart.
It starts at my head,
Reaches down to my feet,
It stretches so I can
Sit down on a seat.
It's got a few freckles
That others can see,
And fingerprint markings
To prove that I'm me.
Skin comes in all sizes
And colours and shades,
And proves, without doubt,
We're all brilliantly made!

Isolated

i

solated

Under pressure

I cheated in the Maths test
And now I have come top;
I'll have to tell the teacher
Or my conscience will go pop!

Hidden

A	P	X	Z	F	G	A	Q
Y	S	O	M	E	X	E	V
O	B	W	H	D	B	W	H
J	Y	T	H	I	N	G	S
N	C	M	I	R	U	J	V
Z	I	N	B	J	C	I	D
T	V	E	K	L	I	F	E
A	F	L	G	N	K	O	L
R	U	M	S	T	P	S	Q
E	H	I	D	D	E	N	R

Detention tension (a rap)

I'm looking at the ceiling,
I'm looking at the wall,
I'm looking at the floor
And I'm feeling very small;
I'm in detention,
Just feel the tension,
Teacher's attention
Is all on me.

I'm sitting at a desk,
I'm sitting very still,
I'm sitting up straight
And I'm feeling sort of ill;
I'm in detention,
Just feel the tension,
Teacher's attention
Is all on me.

I'm writing out lines,
I'm writing very fast,
I'm trying to write neatly,
I don't think it will last;
I'm in detention,
Just feel the tension,
Teacher's attention
Is all on me.

I'm trying to look sorry,
I'm trying to look good,
I'm trying to behave
The way I know I should;
I'm in detention,
Just feel the tension,
Teacher's attention
Is all on me.

Now...
Teacher's looking at the ceiling,
He's looking at the wall,
He's looking at the floor
And I think he's going to call,
'End of detention,
Can't stand the tension,
'Cause your attention
Is all on me!'

A grave decision

Here lies
my dad's
entire wardrobe.

Suddenly slipped away
(when he wasn't looking).

Dead but never forgotten...
we've got the photographs.

A small problem

For the very last day of term
We were told to take in a game,
So I took in my shrinking laser
And decided to practise my aim.

In the middle of assembly,
When the teachers were asleep,
I shrunk the head and deputy,
Put them in a box to keep.

And, when it was time for Music,
Miss Smith got quite a shock
When her old piano stool
Became a tower block.

I helped her to get down,
In case she slipped and fell,
Then I opened up the box
To pop her in as well!

I shrank each teacher in the school
And put them all away
Into my box which I addressed,
'To St Mary's PTA'.

The PTA won't know about
My expert shrinking craft,
But they'll soon find out, without a doubt,
That our school is too short-staffed!

Cornered

They chased me to the corner of the playground,
Where the air is colder
Because spiteful gusts of wind rush at the chain-link
   fence,
And dust blows in your face, rubs like sandpaper.

One tear escaped – then all was lost.
In for the kill, their teeth flashed through parted lips,
Their eyes narrowed in contempt.
I stared at the tarmac, cornered.

Rhymed insults sang a sneering song around my head
And 'Baby! Baby! Baby!' boxed my ears
Until I was on the ground,
My fingers spread over my face like prison bars.

90° safety

I
stand
in the corner
of the playground
because the two walls
protect me better than one

The world is dark when all my friends go cold (a villanelle*)

The world is dark when all my friends grow cold,
And icy stares show no sign of a thaw,
And even Ben believes the lies he's told.

The gossip is protected like it's gold
And each will add to it a little more;
The world is dark when all my friends grow cold.

The hurtful lies soon grow a hundredfold.
I hear my name when passing by each door,
And even Ben believes the lies he's told.

Now all the fragile memories I hold
Of loyal friends are broken on the floor;
The world is dark when all my friends grow cold.

I realize my secrets have been sold,
My heart is rubbed with sadness 'til it's raw.
And even Ben believes the lies he's told.

Mum says that I must learn to be more bold,
Dad says life's tough, I have to know the score;
But the world is dark when all my friends grow cold,
And even Ben believes the lies he's told.

*A villanelle has five three-lined verses and a final verse of four lines.
Line one and line three are repeated in a special pattern – can you work it
out? These two lines always come together to finish the poem off. What
rhyme pattern can you see?

School concert

Abdul's mum is coming,
Nathan's dad appears,
Sofia's nan's in the front row
Because she just can't hear.

Harry's parents always come
Just like Natalie's,
Paul's aunt wouldn't miss it –
And she always smiles at me.

Gemma's mum's brought Thomas –
The baby brother from hell,
Who will scream at the wrong moment,
Then wriggle and stamp and yell.

Hannah's sister, Rachel,
Is sitting near the door
So she can nip out quickly,
Get back to work by four.

And I stare at the door
In hope that I will see
Someone arrive to cheer and clap
Especially for me.

Nativity in 20 seconds

Silent night
Candle light
Holy bright

Stable poor
Prickly straw
Donkey snore

Babe asleep
Lambs leap
Shepherds peep

Star guide
Kings ride
Manger side

Angels wing
Bells ring
Children sing
WELCOME KING!

Proposal at the school council

In the playground
(Overnight)
I'd like to put
A few things right.
In one corner
I would make
A burger bar
For morning break.

Then by the bins
(Made spotless, clean)
I'd make a great big
Cinema screen.
Next to the wall
With the water fountain,
I'd pile up cushions
Like a mountain.
Then I'd cleverly
Rig the clock
So that, at playtime,
Time would stop.
Of course, for winter,
I'd fit a roof –
Retractable
And waterproof.
I hope you think
These alterations
Won't cause too much
Altercation!

Onions are just like me, you have to peel before you see the many layers deep inside, the parts of me I always hide

A visit to casualty

In casualty there's a nurse with 'Jesus fingers' –
She touches gently and strokes away pain.
She has long, calming fingers –
As delicate as spider silk,
Smoothed at the ends by acts of kindness.
Each finger is clean, but some are marked,
Scarred by years of caring.

Her fingers are strong, you can depend on them.
They hold tightly to your hand as you walk down
     to X-ray,
They firmly cradle your head when the doctor prods.
If you cry, you can be sure one of those fingers
Will dry your tears.

They are fingers that steady you if you lose your
     balance,
They play games with you to make you smile.
They softly lift strands of hair away from your eyes
And carefully wash dirt from the sore bits.

Grown-ups probably won't notice her Jesus fingers
'Cause they find it hard to see through the eyes of
     their spirit,
They don't like to be touched by the unusual.

It was your time

You had to leave, it was your time.
But the large space you've left behind
Is not cold and full of sadness –
Instead it echoes with warm laughter,
With funny stories and well worn jokes.
Everywhere around I see and hear small reminders
That once a big man with a soft heart
Walked under the same sky as me.

l look around your workshop
Where tools now sleep, bedded in dust.
I skip through fields edged with poplar trees,
As straight as soldiers,
Until I reach the oak tree you helped me climb.
And I smile at local boys playing football,
Knowing that you would have scored better goals.

But you had to leave, it was your time.
So you slipped away gently
Wearing that calm smile of faith,
Like a saint whose mission was completed.

Tears

tears

sting

and

drip

one

at

a

time

down

my

face

all

alone

In a country churchyard

Sam shepherd's below,
When rounding up sheep
He swallowed his whistle,
Now he can't make a peep.

Here lies the body
Of school marm Blye,
But she can still see you
With her X-ray eye!

Here lies the immaculate
Mrs O'Keefe,
Dressed in her hat, her pearls
And her teeth.

Farmer Brown's grave
Is deep and long
To fit in the tractor
He died upon.

Bob crafted beautiful candles,
He never ever muffed it,
One day he made his best one yet
But then, alas, he snuffed it.

Here lies the wife
Of Archie, the miller,
Some say she did slip,
Some say he did kill 'er.

Witch hunt

We knew she lived at number 89 –
The 'witch-woman' they talked about.
And many times we passed her gate,
Craning our necks to look through
The crack in her curtains.

At night it was more exciting;
Fear jumped around in our stomachs,
And, if her door opened, we ran,
Hearts pounding, to the end of the road.

One night we made a sport of her,
Knocked her door and hid.
Too scared to move, too scared to breathe,
We waited to see her ugliness.

But her nose wasn't pointed,
Her skin was clear,
And she stared sadly
With a tired smile of forgiveness.

'Don't believe everything you hear,' she said timidly,
And I felt the blush of shame.

Morning tongue untwister

When I wake up in the morning
My eyes are full of mist,
My hair is like a breaking wave
And my tongue is in a twist.

'Morning!' shouts Mum,
'Ugh!' I reply, as my tongue flops into a heap.
'Breakfast is ready!' she says urgently.

My tongue searches around my mouth
For a few useful syllables,
Then gropes its way towards 'Exit.'
"ust 'oming,' I breathe out.
'Don't go back to sleep!' Mum pleads.
Then silence.
Sleepily I grab hold of the end of my tongue,
Smooth out the twists and folds, and shake it hard.

On the back of a yawn, familiar sounds tumble out
In a colourful hubbub of wakefulness,
Rushing me into the rhythm of daytime.

Well, well, well

This well is well-deep,
You wouldn't feel well if you fell down there.
The bottom is well-dark,
Bet the mud is well-soft,
Be over the top of your wellies!
I'd be well-gutted if I lost something down there,
I'd be well-fed up,
I'd feel, well, you know.

My aunt, the well-spoken one
From Motherwell, well-bred,
Told me once, 'Don't play near a well
Because the walls are well-worn.'
Well, she meant well,
Only interested in my well-being.

My dad told me, and he's well-informed,
That well-behaved children
Don't play in dilapidated, decaying places.
He says they have more sense,
Being well-balanced individuals.

So, well, keep well-away from old ruins;
All things wear out eventuwelly,
Even words.

Demolition job

They jumped on our castle – the big, laughing boys.
Then they ran through the middle,
Kicking sand and shells into the air.
We stared down at scattered pebbles,
Refusing to look at their mocking faces.
And then they walked on,
Like extras from a production of *Grease*,
Swaggering and joking, throwing stones at waves.

When we were sure they'd gone,
We crawled back out of ourselves into the
    sunshine.
If a wave had destroyed it, it would have been
    bearable –
The ever-edging-closer tide can't be stopped.
We could have half-celebrated the inevitable,
And paddled amongst the fallen walls and
    turrets.
But this was different; our castle had been
    cheapened into a joke.
They had scoffed at our design and smashed
    our afternoon's fantasy.
Spite had rushed towards us like a tidal wave.

Grandad's pants

Grandad's pants billow on the washing line
Like the enormous sails of an old ship,
Ready to voyage to a distant land –
Maybe they'll sail to the West Undies.

Gum alert

My bubble gum increased its size
Until it covered both my eyes;
The bubble then split into two
And both the bubbles grew and grew;
They lifted me up in my room

Like two enormous gum ball \ ns.
So now I cannot hide from Mum
That, despite her rules, I'm chewing gum!

The hole truth

Mum...
The hole in my trousers isn't my fault,
A stone in the playground was sharp
And it ripped the material quickly,
So the stone really tore them apart.

And I wouldn't have run, but for Jason,
He chased me until I fell down;
He was in such a mood at break time,
I could tell by the depth of his frown.

And he wouldn't have been in a temper
If our teacher had taken it better
When he said he'd forgotten his homework
And then squirted ink on her sweater!

And our teacher would have been a lot calmer
If the head hadn't told her that day
The reports she had left in the office
Had, mistakenly, been thrown away.

So the hole in my trousers isn't my fault,
Or the stone's, or Jason's, or teacher's,
You could say it's the fault of head teacher –
You should make an appointment to see her!

Flat and safe

Mum's had a perm;
Either that or some accident with electricity!
And she likes it.
Her friends like it.
My dad likes it.
But her head looks like an exploding mattress.
She's got more coils than a party full of streamers,
And more bounce than ten kangaroos on
     trampolines!
She says it makes her feel glamorous.
She says I'll get used to it –
But I won't!
She ought to look like Mum,
The way she always used to look,
Flat and safe.

Hair flair

It's so easy to see

It's so easy to tell

If my brother has

Been using hair gel

Acrostics

Acrostics
Clearly
Reveal
Obsessional
Sequencing
Tendencies
In
Clever
So-and-sos

My team

They're a...
Hard-shooting
Firm-booting
Fast-running
Crowd-stunning
Ball-keeping
Nifty-sweeping
Smooth-gliding
Glory-riding
First-rating
Penetrating
Stadium-filling
Opponent-killing
Net-whacking
Post-cracking
Table-topping
Breath-stopping
Drama-making
RECORD-BREAKING
Sort of team!!

Magic feet

I'm no good at spelling,
I'm no good at all,
But my teacher's never there to see
My feet spell with a ball.

My feet spell with a ball, you know,
And people stare at what I do –
Teacher, come and watch me play,
I'll write a goal for you.

Goal difference

with	success
weigh	heavy
the	top
teams	at
but	the
the	table
climb	up
needed	to
the	results
to	get
is	on
the	pressure
the	league
bottom	of
At	the

Clue – poems don't always start at the top.

Writer's block

writer's block

writer's block

writer's block

I've got

writer's block

writer's block